Young Learner's

LEARNING ALPHABET

Airplane

Abacus

Ant

Apple

Bread

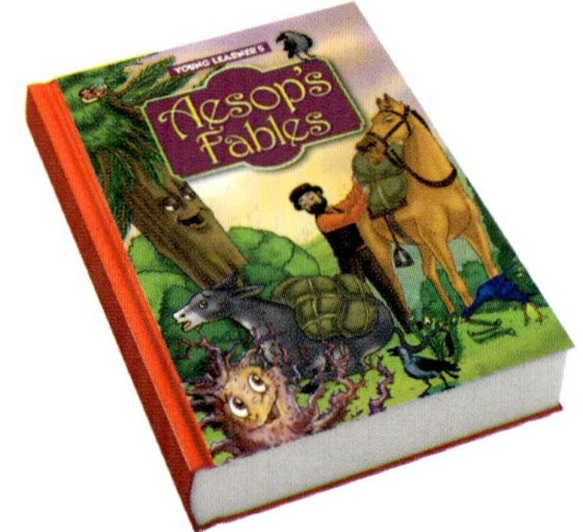

Book

Ball

Baby

Cc
Comb
Cake
Cup
Crayons
Dd
Drum
Doll
Doughnut
Dustbin

Ee

Eraser

Egg

Eagle

Earth

Ff

Frying pan

Fruit cake

Fish

Fan

Gg

Goldfish

Grapes

Gloves

Girl

Hh

Helicopter

Hamburger

Hamster

Honey

Ii

Iguana

Iron

Igloo

Ice cream

Jj

Jaguar

Jacket

Jump rope

Joker

Kk
Kiwi fruit
Kite
Kettle
Koala
Ll
Lute
Lamp
Lock
Lemon

Mm
Mask
Milk
Meerkat
Macaron

Nn
Nuts
Noodles
Napkin
Nest

Oo

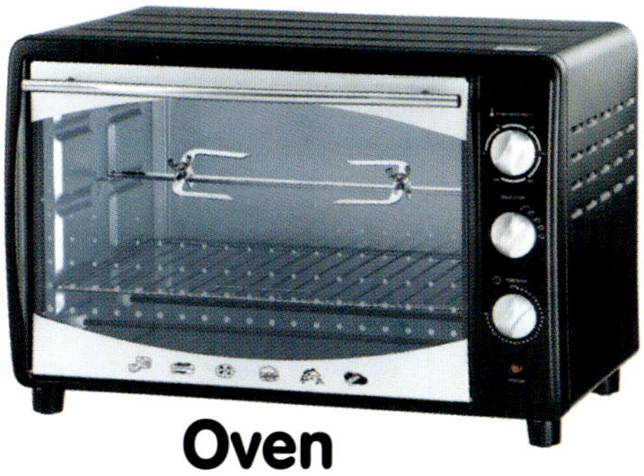

Oven

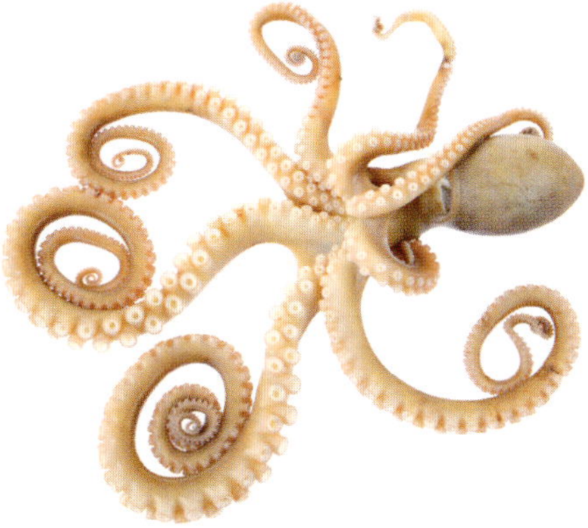

Octopus

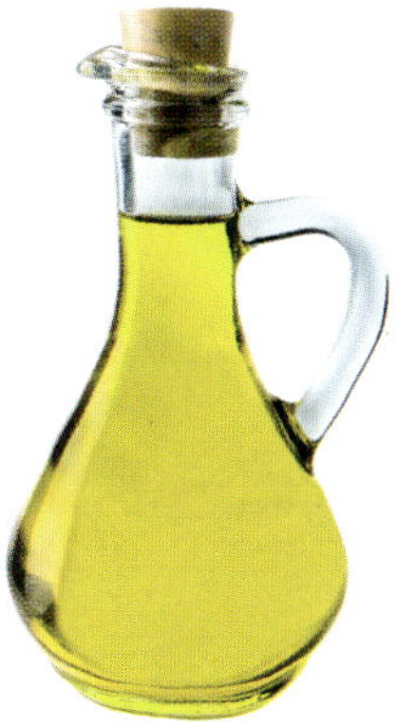

Oil

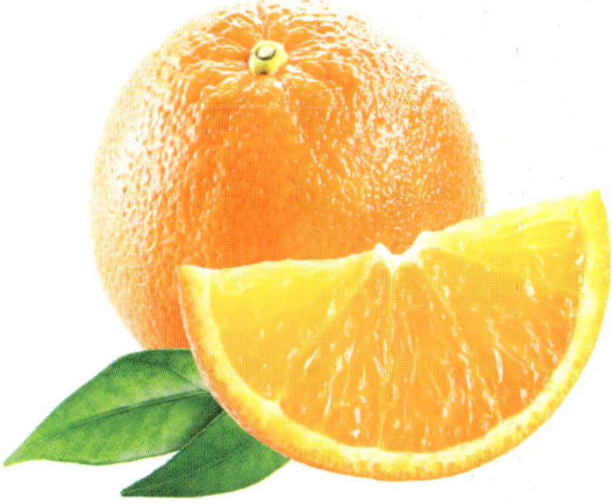

Orange

Pp

Peanut

Pumpkin

Paintbrush

Penguin

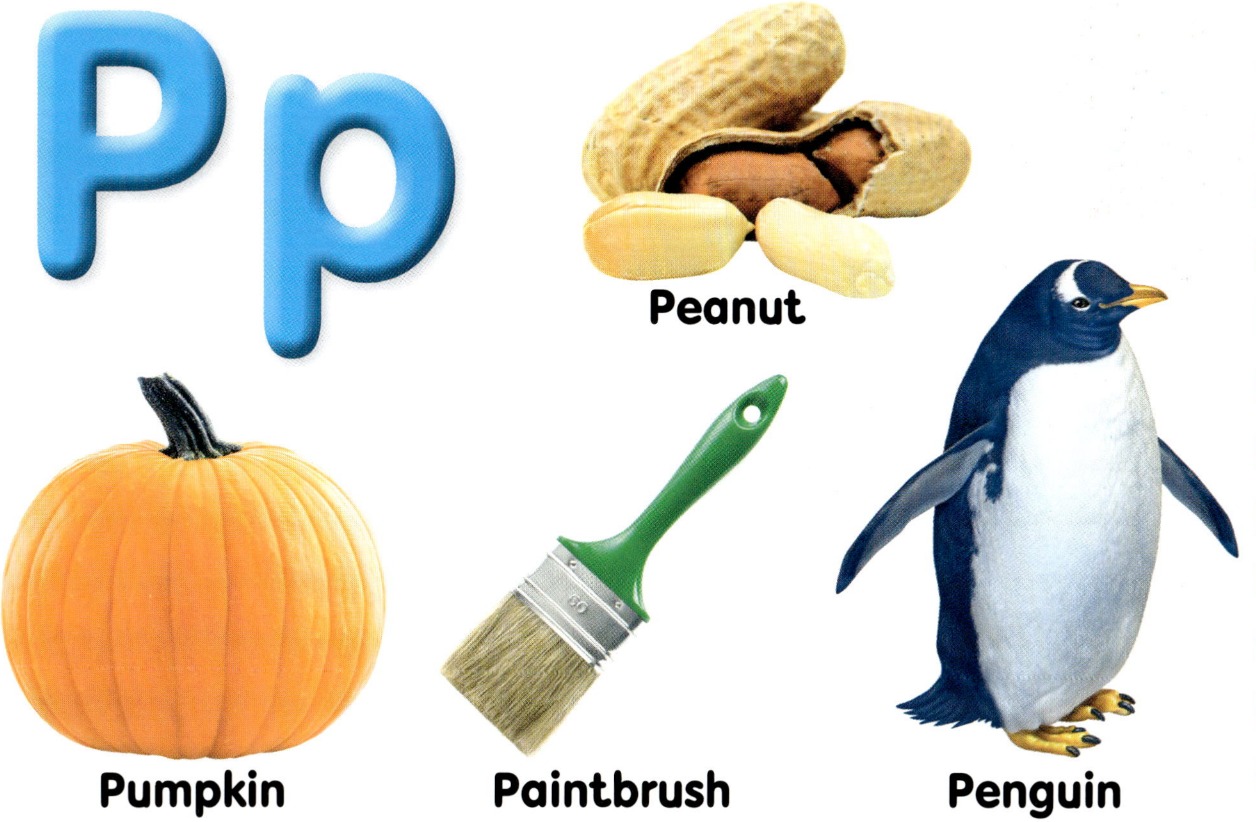

Qq

Queue

Quad bike

Quince

Quilt

Rr

Rat

Rattle

Rocking horse

Robot

Ss
soup
Soup
Squirrel
Saucepan
Seahorse
Tt
Tiger
Tent
Tomato
Tricycle

Uu

Utensils

Uniform

Umbrella

Unicycle

Vv

Villa

Vegetables

Vase

Violin

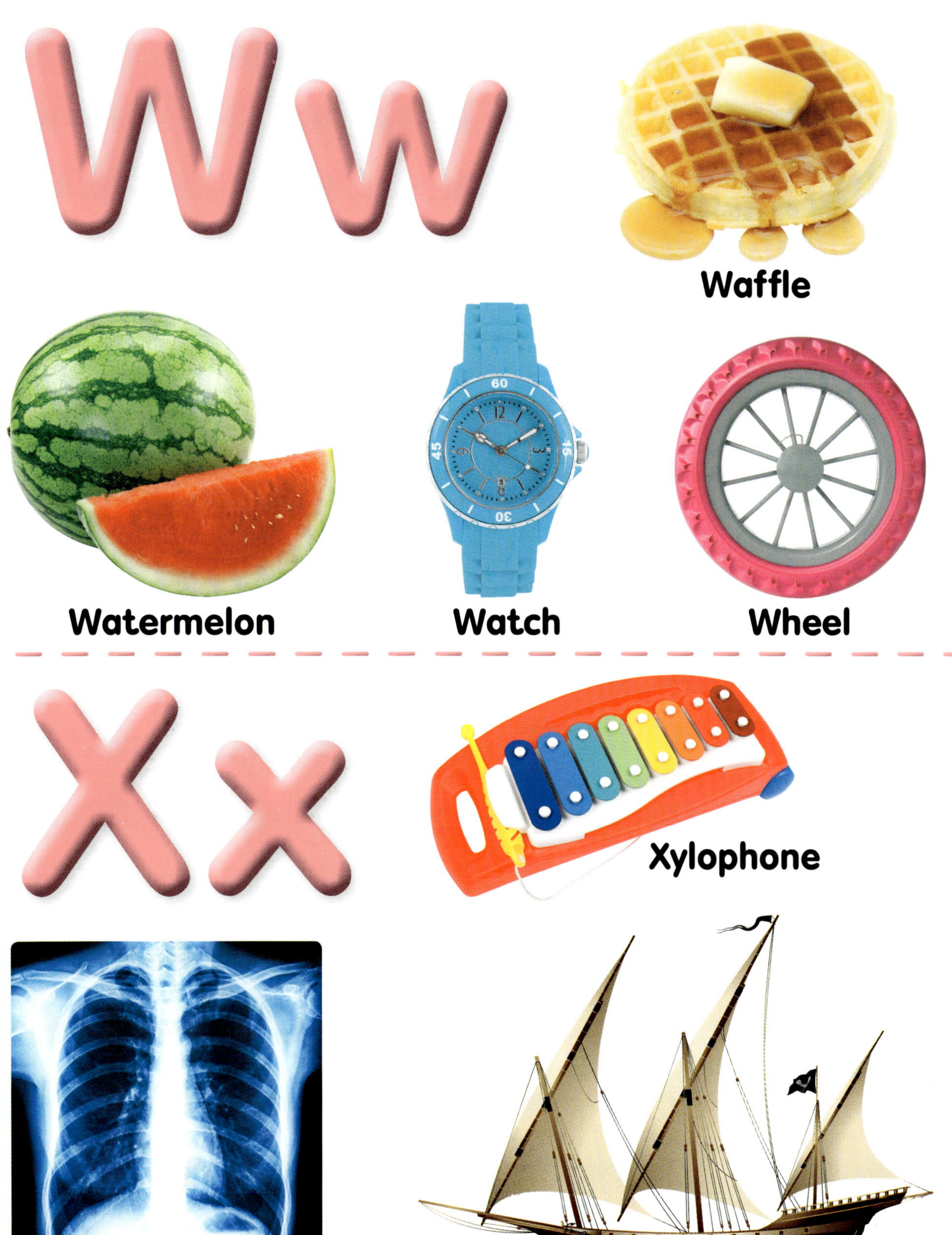
Ww
Waffle
Watermelon
Watch
Wheel
Xx
Xylophone
X-ray
Xebec

Yy
Yak
Yoghurt
Yo-yo
Yule log cake
Zz
Zucchini
Zero
Zinnia flower
Zebra

ACTIVITY TIME!

Match the capital and small letters to the objects.

X	 s
E	 j
N	 x
K	 a
S	 k
A	 n
J	 e

ACTIVITY TIME!

Match the pictures that start with the same alphabet.

Printed in India